I was a

Wife

before you found me

Keaires Roberson

To my brothers, sisters and my loving mother.
I love you all more than you will ever know.
Thank you for believing in me and
pushing me to be the best!

Table of Contents

Introduction   8

Chapter 1
The Good 'Ol Days   13

Chapter 2
Welcome to my Reality   19

Chapter 3
What sis I go and do that for?   27

Chapter 4
Time for a Change   37

Chapter 5
Loving You   49

Chapter 6
What men really want   59

Chapter 7
There is someone
equipped to carry you   71

Chapter 8
Saving It   79

Chapter 9
From the Beginning   93

Introduction

We stayed up all night reminiscing on the good times because we knew our time was coming to an end. I laid my head on his bronze chest, and looked into his one eye, as he caressed my body with his masculine hands. I let him have his way with my body, as I had done so many times before. God kept making a way for me to escape, but

I kept closing the door. I knew this man was bad for me, but I loved him anyway. After a night full of pleasure, I got up early the next morning and cooked what would be his last free meal. Scrambled eggs, biscuits, sausage and grits.

As we sat down on the couch to eat breakfast, he said, "Baby they coming."

I responded, "How you know?"

He stated, "I see them circling the block."

I looked out the blinds to see for myself. Sure enough, police cars were circling the big yellow house. My heart instantly dropped to my toes. There was a loud bang at the door. Boom! Boom! Boom! Boom! The knock at the door grew louder and louder. Boom! Boom! Boom! Boom!

"Open the door or we are in kicking it in, yelled a loud voice on the other side of the door."

I frantically opened the door, to guns of all shapes and sizes pointed in my face.

"Where is he? "Where is he? The man in blue and black yelled.

I stood there scared out of my mind. I was in such shock that I couldn't speak. The policeman snatched me out of the doorway and threw me into the police car. I silently sat and watched the police run into the house and come back out with Twan. They threw him to the ground and handcuffed him. The dogs were barking going crazy! I was crying uncontrollably. As he lay handcuffed on the ground he looked up at me and I peered at him through the police car window. My mind was all over the place. All I could think about at that moment, was what in the hell have I gotten myself into?

Chapter 1

The Good 'Ol Days

I remember it like it was yesterday, sitting in the salon chair getting my 20 inches of weave sowed in. I was known for getting different hairstyles and wearing all types of colors. I remember getting kinky twist one time, (a different name for dreadlocks.) I was so cute, well at least everybody else thought so. This one girl went on and on about how cute my hair was, then later she sneak attacked me and pulled out every single kinky twist. Ol hater! I was mad as hell. I spent good money to get that hair. But the joke was on her, I got it redone the very next day. So, I was back fine like nothing ever happened. But I got my tail whooped! Ya girl was not a fighter. A trophy yes, but definitely not a fighter. I traveled from Sheffield to Huntsville to buy an outfit just to go to the club. I would not be caught dead looking like anyone else. I made sure I was in the club every single weekend, just to see the same people I saw every single day. Foolish right? The pre-turn up was so real. I would spend the evening making drinks at my friend's house. Just call me the bartender. You name it, I could mix it, even if there was not a name for it, I could still mix it. Yes! I was that good. Who wants a drink with no food? Not me! My aunt helped raised me, so I was always in the kitchen cooking. I was a beast in the kitchen. Not to toot my own horn, but to this day, I am still a beast in the kitchen. When we were not at my friend's house, we were at my house partying non-stop. My house was the hangout, kick it spot. No matter who you were, you were welcomed. Once the pre-game was over, we made our way to the club. Most of the time we did not have enough money, because we spent it on hair, nails and new outfits, so we made sure we made it to the club free before 11 pm. We knew we would get drinks once we got inside the club, as we always did. I recall waiting in that long line, freezing, shaking, but I was fine though! When we finally got inside the club it was empty except for the other women who needed to get in free, but slowly the men began to come and that is when the drinks started. If the drinks did not come soon enough, no worries I would blackmail "Twan".

"Buy me and my friends some drinks or I will make a scene." I would tell him.

Because he had multiple women, the last thing he wanted was for me to make a scene, so he always bought the drinks. After about 4 drinks, I began to feel myself. The dance floor became my way to escape every time. My escape from life and pain that I held quietly inside of my heart. Once my friends saw me heading toward the dance floor they would yell Ciara 'finna get it. Ciara was my nickname because I knew all of Ciara's music and dance moves. I stepped in front of the mirror and twirled my hips. The dance floor and I became one. I would dance for hours and hours until the club closed, and they turned on the lights. I remember feeling sad once they flipped the lights on. A deep part of me knew reality had set back in and it was time to get back to life.I

Chapter 2

Welcome to my reality

"Pootyyyy!" my mom yelled, "I have to work a double shift, and I need you to watch your brothers and sisters.

"Huhhhh" I mumbled under my breath, as I laid in my bed.

Yep back to my reality. My life, which I hated.

"I swear I am not having any kids," was my famous quote for most of my life.

Growing up, I was the eldest of six. I pretty much raised my brothers and sisters, and for that reason, I was sure I did not want kids of my own. No matter where I went or what I did, one of my siblings was always with me. I tried my best to protect them. I was their protector. My sister called it the "Save a Sibling" trip. My mom had bad judgment when choosing men, and I hated most of them. They were monsters! I felt like they sought us, like when a lion is searching for prey. They viewed my mother as a weak opponent. As if our house had a sign in the yard that read, perverts, rapists, drunks, abusers you are welcomed here. My baby sister became so attached to my hip, that people thought she was my child. I began to despise my mother. I despised her for leaving us at home with her no-good boyfriend or whoever was there at the time. I despised her for trusting these deranged men with her children. The men always came first. I felt as if my word was never good enough for my mother. I used to always ask myself when I will be good enough for my mother. I felt as if nothing I did or said was good enough for her and like I was not worthy of even being her daughter. My mom worked multiple jobs. Since I was the eldest, I was always left in charge. It taught me a set of skills that I would soon need, how to be a mother. I always had to cook and clean. It was so nerve-racking. I was only 17 years old, but one thing I was sure of. Is that I was sick and tired of being an adult. I felt as if I had been an adult my whole life. The way I escaped adulthood was to be in somebody's club every Saturday and sometimes Friday nights. The club helped to take my mind off the constant thoughts that haunted me day and night. I knew the only time I would be free of responsibility was at the club. One drink quickly escalated to ten. I hated being sober. Being sober was a painful place for me.

When I was drunk, the constant movie of being raped as a child did not play in my mind. The T.V. would become blurry and static. The DVD player in my head only worked when I was sober. As long as I was dancing and drinking, the DVD player would skip the parts of my mom being physically abused. It skipped the part of my brothers and sisters standing at the top of the stairs, crying and yelling get up mama get up, as she lay helpless on the floor, after being thrown down a flight of stairs. It skipped the part of her being choked and held against the wall, as we watched helplessly not being able to do anything about it. It skipped the part of me as a little girl lying in bed under all white sheets naked, scared of what was about to happen next. It skipped the part of the grown man climbing under those same white sheets, to finish what he started.

It skipped the part of 9-year-old me standing in the bathroom mirror whimpering, in pain, ready for the nightmare to end. It skipped the part of the grown man down on his knees, performing oral on little girl me. The DVD player skipped the parts of me crying silently in bed, because I didn't know who I was, and I felt as if I deserved to have my innocence stripped away from me. Although, my soberness was painful drunkenness brought me peace. At least when I was drunk, the DVD player powered off.

Chapter 3

What did I go and do that for?

Power on. Once again I found myself sleeping with someone else's man Shoot the way I saw it, no one ever spared my feelings when I was in a relationship, so I was done sparing theirs. I went from one bad relationship to another. Well, not all bad, my previous relationship before Twan may not have lasted but I gained an amazing gift, my son. I know previously I said I was not having any kids, but I messed around and got caught slipping. My Baby Daddy was also somebody's man when I met him by the way. I did not know who I was, which resulted in not knowing who I needed to be with. I had just gotten out of a long-term relationship with my son's father, so I should have been healing, but instead, I was doing what I did the best drinking and clubbing away all my problems. This never worked, by the way.

One night I was at my friend's house, and her cousin walked in. Twan spoke, I spoke, I did not think much afterward. Then the fisherman threw his hook, to see if I would bite. My friends and family warned me "Do not talk to him! Do not do it!" They knew the man behind the mask. In the beginning, I would not talk to him, no matter how hard he tried. However, the vulnerability made me, the fish, bite. I saw potential in him, and I thought I could change him. So, I thought. In the beginning, he wined and dined me. He whispered sweet nothings in my ear. We had a great conversation, which was something I was not use to. My previous relationship with my Baby Daddy was cold and full of silence. Granted he was a great provider. When we lived together he paid all the bills, made sure everything was in order. But Twan spoiled me, treated me like a princess. I felt like I was on cloud nine. I soon discovered the drug dealing life styled he lived. But that did not matter to me. He would tell me he was ready to get out of the streets and give up that lifestyle. I was the one he was going to change for. I was the one he was going to straighten up and fly right for. He had finally met the girl of his dreams and I had finally met the man of my dreams. After months of not caving into his real agenda, it happened. We slept together. This is when everything began to unravel.

It did not take long before I began to find out about other women that he was seeing. When he was with me his phone rang constantly, and it was not because he was making drug deals. I recall him sitting on the side of the bed, trying to be discreet when he had a call. I heard a woman's voice on the other end.

"Where are you?"

"I need my hair did."

"I need my nails did."

"When are you bringing me some money?"

It was always a different voice.

When I would see his other women out in public, if I did not know who they were, they would make it their business to make sure from that point I did. They would see me and roll their eyes or smirk at me. I had never been so intimidated in my life. In addition to the women, the long romantic conversations stopped. It turned into drop-offs and booty calls. I felt like his hoe! How did this happen?

Soon his true crazy began to show. He would beat people who owed him money, cook, sell, and hide dope all in front of me. I was at his house one night, sitting on the couch in the living room. I heard a lot of commotion coming from the kitchen. Then I heard him yelling and asking where was his money. I knew how upset he became when it came to his money, so whoever the person was in the kitchen needed to pay up quick! I continued to sit quietly on the couch, I knew better to intervene. He walked into the living room grabbed the statue off the table, which was about the size of a lamp, then went back into the kitchen. I could hear the licks sounding off the walls. I began shaking with fear of seeing a large amount of blood everywhere. I ran into the back bedroom because I did not want to be a witness to anything. No matter how hard I tried to stay out of his drama, it always found its way to me.

I was at my cousin house one day sitting on the bed talking to her. We heard a loud bang at the door. It was him standing there in a white t-shirt drenched in blood. He barged straight past us and made his way into the house. We both started freaking out.

"What's going on? What did you do?", we exclaimed.

He just kept pacing back and forth. He handed my cousin his dope and gun and said hide this for me. He said the police were after him. He hid at my cousin's house for a short time, then out of nowhere he jumped up and ran out the back door. We later found out he had beat up one of the girls he was dating. When I found this out all kinds of thoughts ran through my mind. "Why run to me?" I know as you are reading this you want to know if he ever beat me? No! He never put his hands on me. I do not know if it was the grace of God saving me, or that I threatened to tell the police his hiding spots if he ever laid a finger on me. But since we are being honest, the other females always received more, more of his time, more of his money, vacations, hair, new outfits, shoes, whatever they wanted. I used to be sad when I found out what he did for them and not me. I felt as if I was the peasant. Then I also rejoiced, because if I had to take a black eye and a bruised face, I will take the 100 Alex. Why didn't I leave? Well, I was in too deep. As crazy and messed up as he was, I loved him. Even when I tried to stop seeing him I could not. He was like a bad cold I could never get rid of. I ended up with exactly what I said I never would. A baddddd boy!

Chapter 4

Time for a change

A bad boy indeed is what I had, but not all parts of him were bad. I could see the good in him, but potential alone was not enough. Deep down in my heart, I knew it was time for a change. My life was in shambles. I was going nowhere fast. After being homeless, living from house to house, I found myself carless and walking in the snow with a baby on one hip and groceries in the other hand. I then knew it was time for a change. I was sick and tired of being sick and tired. I was not the most stable person. I lived with my baby daddy when we were together, his parents. Then my aunt, cousin, friend, whoever would open their doors. I did not have the best of luck when it came to cars. I was so gullible when it came to men. I ended up carless because my baby daddy gave me a car while we were together. But once he found out I was talking to Twan he took the car from me. Geesh I know right. And to make matters worse, Twan gave me a car, and his side pieces put sugar and candy bars in the tank. So, there I was carless again. I could not win for losing.

It was time for Keaires to put the fast life down, step up and be a mother. When my son was a toddler he was always in New Orleans with his grandparents, which caused me to miss a lot of his milestones. I missed his first step, I missed him losing his first tooth. I loved him, but apparently, I loved the streets more. I recently had a conversation with my sister reflecting on my past, "I remember when I use to live in the projects and I did not have a comforter set on my bed or any sheets. I just had a big cover, a borrowed cover at that."

It made me sad, to know my priorities were that jacked up. Because of that experience, I now have multiple comforter sets and several big covers. To some, that may seem small, but once you have been deprived of something for so long, you tend to appreciate it more. I remember blowing large amounts of money on food, liquor, hair, and nails. Whenever I would go out to eat, the liquor cost on my tab alone would be three times the price I paid for my food. I would leave work and rush to the liquor store to buy a bottle. I would get a loan after loan. Twan convinced me to get a Title loan on the car he bought for me. He said he would pay it back but left me stuck with the bill. It seemed like a good idea, the car did not work properly after one of his women stuffed candy bars in the gas tank. I would get loans for jewelry. Jewelry that I wanted, or jewelry for whomever I was dealing with at the time. Loans for men. Loans just because I could. I was young and did not realize getting those loans would affect my credit. All I knew is that I needed the money and the loan people were available. My days begin to turn into nights and my nights to days. I felt empty inside. With Twan gone, I felt like I had nothing left. My mother called me one day and said: "Pooty come home". Come live in Huntsville with me."

That's exactly what I did. Moving to Huntsville, Alabama was the best decision of my life. As I much as I disliked my mother in the past. I loved her all the more, for encouraging me to move out of my hometown of Sheffield, Alabama. The love for my mother began to grow and the hate dwindled away. I began to see a different side of her. She began to push and motivate me to do better. I was starting to feel like I now had her approval. That I was finally enough for my mother now. I guessed her moving helped her grow as well. Making the decision to leave a toxic environment was very beneficial for me, and it catapulted me into "my next". I imagine God was saying "Okay Pooty, you've had your fun, it is time to get serious about your life." It didn't happen immediately and it took a while for me to follow suit, but eventually got it together. I began to break old habits and started new ones. I started going to church and got to know God for real for real. Sometimes we resist change because we do not understand it, or we have gotten too comfortable with our norm.

"See, I am doing a new thing! Now it springs up; do you not perceive it? I am making a way in the wilderness and streams in the wasteland."
Isaiah 43:19 NIV

God knew he had to bring forth change in my life. He knew if he left it up to me, I would have taken everybody with me. God began to have me cut certain people off and others just fell off. He changed the diagram of people that I surrounded myself with. I had to stop certain things I had been entertaining, no more club hoping, no more boyfriends, no more house parties and mixing up my famous drinks. Well, let's just say my new circle of friends does not do those things anyway. The people I am now connected to pray for me. We do not club together, we do life together. They pull what's in me out of me. And they encourage me to do and be my very best. When I became wiser I began to pay off loans and invest in myself. I started my business, Key-Plays where I help others tap into their God-given purpose through fasting, prayer, and self-reflection. This information can be obtained at Key-Plays.teachable.com. God has allowed me to speak on multiple platforms, encouraging and uplifting women just like you and me. I also wrote my first book, entitled 5am with God which seeks to aid people in building a closer relationship with God.

My struggles and situations taught me if I cannot afford something do not buy it. When I go into a store now I take the advice of a very wise woman, Maleeka Hollaway, and I ask myself is it a want, need or investment? I very seldom borrow money, because borrowing means you must pay it back. God placed me around people in higher tax brackets than mine. I found myself going to lunch with very influential people. He brought people who pushed me in every area of my life. They push me to pray more, work out, and seek God. My old friends did not do that. I am now convinced they did not know how. He sent new people who have helped me flourish into the beautiful butterfly, that I am today.

Dear Best Friend

This poem is dedicated to one of my old friends.

*Dear Best Friend, I hope you know that I
miss you and I think about you every day.
At night I use to cry and ask God isn't
there another way.
It was nothing you did or did not do.
There were some things I had to deal with.
It was me and not you!
He did not have me cut you off, but me cut
off from you.
I was no good at the time, intoxicating,
killing me and you.
Sure, we had fun, drinking, partying till the
sun came up. But there was a little voice in
me telling me it was time for me to give
that life up.
I pray one day our paths will cross again.
Out of all the friends I have ever had.
You are the one I cannot seem to get past.
Know when I make it that means you make
it too.
No matter what we have been through.
Always remember Best friend I love you!*

Chapter 5

Loving you

For a long time in my life, I did not love myself. To be honest I did not know how. I have learned from my past that not knowing how to properly love myself, made it impossible for me to effectively love anyone else. What I thought was love, was really me tripping over the same untied shoelaces. It was not love, but really insecurities. I would do whatever I felt would be pleasing to someone else, even if it meant hurting me. I was a do girl, a yes person. I had every right to be. I learned to be submissive at a very young age, so it just spilled over into adulthood. Whatever people expected of me, I did it. If my man wanted me and his other chick to spend the night, fine, she was not leaving and neither was I. If he wanted us both in the kitchen cooking, cool, I was with it. If bae wanted a threesome, sure why not? Might as well. I thought that was love. It must have been love. Wrong! Nothing about that was love.

What did I really know about love anyway? It was never expressed in our home. I cannot recall a time where my brothers and sisters and I kissed one another or my mom. It was a very foreign act. As we have gotten older we are working to change how we express our feelings toward each other.

Love is patient, love is kind. It does not envy, it does not boast, it is not proud. It does not dishonor others, it is not self-seeking, it is not easily angered, it keeps no record of wrongs. Love does not delight in evil but rejoices with the truth. It always protects, always trusts, always hopes, always perseveres." 1 Corinthians 13:4-7 NIV

My falling in love with me was not an easy task. It was not until I fell in love with God, that I was able to love myself and those around me. God loved on me in a way I had never experienced before, and with his love, forgiveness came. Forgiveness toward the ones who hurt me, as well as my mom. The closer I got to God, the deeper my love for my mom grew. I began to get to know her. The more I found out about her, the more I realized I had been living with a stranger the entire time. She never experienced real love either, similar to me she did know hurt and abuse. She endured and suffered a lot in her lifetime, even as a child. I recall being at an event, and she shared a poem she had written. She revealed so much in the poem, that it brought me to tears. However, that is her story to tell, and I am waiting for the day when she does just that. I know the hell she experienced on earth and it has made me appreciate her. I began to pray and fast for my mother. Sometimes I would go days without eating, spending time in the presence of God, on my mother's behalf. I wanted nothing more than our relationship to be mended.

I remember how I would invite her to my church all the time. She would say "Nope, I am Church of Christ." Then one day she came. One Sunday turned into two until she was coming regularly. I was so happy, I rejoiced. One Sunday while we were attending service I kept trying to leave early because I had a meeting to attend. My cousin came to church with us that day, and she kept saying do not leave. Slightly confused, I remained. I kept thinking if I left a few minutes early it was not going to make a difference.

When my Pastor did the three calls, Baptism, re-connect with Christ or partner with the church. My mom slowly inched out of her seat and made her way to the front. Now I must have not been paying attention, because when I looked up, there she was standing at the front, giving her life to God. And becoming a member of the very church she said she was not coming to. I barely made it to the front, before I hit the ugliest cry in the world. My mouth was open, and I was slobbering everywhere. I bet people were like it does not take all of that. But for me it did, they did not know how long I had been praying and seeking God for that day. It was God's love that brought us to that point. That is when I began to realize that I could not live without God's love or self-love.

Yes, it was a process, but an amazing experience. Since this chapter is titled Loving you, let's talk about that for a moment. You must remember you are your own person. No one's situation is alike. You cannot live for everybody else. If it makes you unhappy, do not do it. Ask yourself what do you like? What do you not like? Do you want kids? Do you even like kids? I know these questions may sound a bit selfish. But nobody should love you more than you. Take those self-care days. You deserve it! Go get a massage, go get your nails done, spend a day at the spa, read a book. Unplug and unwind from the world. If you do not enjoy spending time with you, why would anyone else? Take yourself out on dates. Especially the movies, you do not have to worry about anyone spoiling the movie for you. Dinner for one is a lot cheaper. Get to know you. When is the last time you tried a new food? Travel and go see the world.

We don't have to wait until marriage to enjoy life. Enjoy your life now while you are single. Do single people stuff! Eat cereal for dinner while sitting on the couch in your PJs. Trying to love someone else without first loving you. It is like pouring from an empty glass expecting something to come out. There is nothing in to pour out. I promise you if you spend time with you, you will begin to fall in love with yourself. That broken girl you read about in previous chapters, had to find herself. Finding all while loving yourself before you get married is the best thing you could ever do for you and your mate. Spending time in the presence of God helped me. Going to therapy helped me. Draw close to God and He will show you who you are. If you need additional references on what God's love looks like, grab my first book "5 am With God" at www.keairesroberson.com, and once you know your worth and value you will stop giving your pearls to swine.

Chapter 6

What men really want

After a few relationships went wrong, and lessons learned, I learned from my mistakes and took ownership of where I went wrong. Men like a woman who can admit when she is wrong. Whaaaaattttt?! Yeah, I said it, we are not always right! I began to dig deep, to find out what it is men really want. I can honestly say my past relationships taught me a thing or two. They taught me what men want, what they expect, and how to know when a man is fully and ready to commit. As well as when he is not ready to commit. When a man is ready to be with you and only you there is no devil in hell that can stop him from getting to you. Men are very territorial and dominant. Most men see what they want and go after it. If he is not calling, texting or checking on you. It is because he does not want to. Period! Nobody is that busy sis! Nobody! Even if he is that busy, he will create time for the one he wants to be with. I know a guy, extremely busy, he dealt with different women at the same time, but there was one he truly cared for. He went out of his way to make time for her, even when it meant neglecting other things and responsibilities. Now no, that may have not been the healthy way of doing things, but it showed who he wanted to be with. It did not take rocket science to figure it out.

I also learned a real man does not want a weak woman. I was once a weak woman, which is why I attracted dominating men, who wanted to rule over me. This led me to suffer from identity issues. As I recall every guy that I have been involved with, all apart from one. Felt as if they had to be in control over every little thing. Your God sent husband will not want a "jelly back" woman who cries every time something goes wrong or cannot think for herself.

No one wants to put up with that. A man wants a woman who knows how to take charge and knows what she wants. In the process of finding myself, I killed the yes girl. I became a woman who can make sound decisions on her own. While all of that is true, men still want their lady to be a lady. Let the men handle business, as in be the provider, they want to give you the best. Stand down ladies we are not the man of the house! Even in your single stages, you are not the man of the house and neither is your son. God is the man of the house until you marry your husband. A man wants a whole woman, it is not his job to fix us. Whatever voids we have should be filled before going into a marriage. In my opinion, this is something we should work on in our season of singleness. A married woman once told me, do not keep it sexy for the world then make your husband come home to a bonnet, and set it off braids. According to the men I have spoken with. They hate it! I had a guy tell me nothing makes him more upset than seeing his woman dressed really nice in public, hair did all up, makeup just right and then when he makes it home from work, she has a grandma housecoat on, rollers in her head, and a mud mask.

He said: "I wished she would have just slid on some nice lingerie just for me. versus me having to come home and see that every day." Ouch! I know I am guilty as charged. Though I do not have a man to come home to right now.

Maybe I should start practicing. Keep in mind men hurt, just like women hurt. If you know you are not ready for marriage or have no intention of getting married then do not lead him on. What did your mama tell you growing up? "Don't play with your food! Somebody else could have eaten that." Same with a man, do not waste a good man. Somebody else could have had him. Most men do not like drama, nagging, high pitch yelling for no reason. They desire peace. Men you want her to be your peace, well don't leave her in pieces.

Let me just say it again for those in the back! I can be your peace, just don't leave me in pieces. I did a recent survey at a local barbershop and I asked them do men really want? It was not sex, it was not a big booty nor big boobs. They said, and I quote "we just want to feel appreciated." Wow! Not the answer you were expecting right? Yeah me either. They said after a long day of work, they do not want to hear of their shortcomings and what they need to do better. They want to feel valued. They want to feel loved and needed. Like, let me know you appreciate me paying the bills. Not my words, this came straight out of their mouths. Women I know we like to talk, but after a long day of hard work, most men do not want to hear a never-ending rant. When you listen to respond, you are really not listening at all. Men enjoy affirmation. It is okay to stroke his ego sis. Let him know he is looking good today. Speak into his life. How was your day King? The world beats them down already, especially our black men, it is up to us to make them know they are needed. It is our job to let them know we love them.

Men also desire submission. Of course, you knew that was coming. I believe society has confused submission with slavery. They are not the same! Slavery is forcing you to do something against your will, with little to no pay. If you are in slavery and you rebel for no reason, severe consequences may follow. Submission is not being told what to do or having to follow every instruction someone gives you. Being submitted is following your husband as he follows Christ. Period. If he is not following the vision of God, then sis I am sorry to be the bearer of bad news, but you have nothing to follow. Men, if you want your wife to submit to you must be someone that she trusts. Listen to her ideas and her inputs. Remember she is your help mate, she is there to compliment you. She is not there to be your doormat or to be stepped on and stepped over.

Why Did You Stop Praying For Me?

I stopped praying for you a long time ago! I'm really not sure why?
Maybe because I had given up hope.
The hopes of you finding me seemed slim to none.
I don't know if you got lost or what. But what in the hell, are you waiting on?
Is God hiding you from me? Like Adam and Eve did when they ate the fruit from the tree?
If that's not the case then why haven't you found me?
Am I not pretty enough, am I not your type?
Are you blind?
Do you need glasses?
Now that I think about it, are you even equipped to carry the masses?
I'm not your regular girl, I am a spiritual being living in an earthly world.
I hate what my Father hates. And I despise what He despises.
I love what He loves, and I worship from above!
I bring Heaven to earth; do you even know what that means?
I am Queen sent from above. But yet I still remain a Queen without a King.
Have you been spending time with the Father? Do you even know how to treat me?
I refuse to accept anything less, I won't go beneath me.
And nawl I ain't bragging, I'm just a daddy's girl.
When God found me, He showed me, real love.

He showed me just how a wife should be treated!
Then I began to ask myself, do you really want to
be married?
Do you really want to share your bed?
Well yeah, sometimes I do. I get lonely ya know,
ya girl has needs.
But then I ask myself again, are you even capable
of fulfilling my needs!
Anybody can lay the pipe, and knock off some
proper!
Are you a babe in Christ? Cause if so it will never
work. I gotta few questions for you? When I see
demons at night, will you take flight or stay and
fight.
When I fall into a deep depression because I'm
worn out from life. Will you lift me up, or look at
me with judgmental eyes, shaking your head,
saying this can't be right!
When I tell you what the Lord is saying 5 years
from now concerning the future. Will you believe
me or have me locked in a mental psyche ward?
Oooh oooh, what about when God calls me to the
carpet to go on a 3 day fast with no water and no
food. What! Will you do? Can you cover me?
Is petty arguments your thing? If so there's the
door.
90% of my life I'm here on earth but operating in
the spirit, do you even know what that looks like?
The journey I travel is a very lonely one, can you
withstand it?
Do you know the difference between Revelation
and Illumination?

Are you jelly back or a real man?
If you compromise with the enemy on earth, that's
how you fight in the spirit.
And if you are jelly back you need a mentor at this
stage in your life! Not A Wife!!!
I can not babysit you! I need you to back me. If
you can't do any of this, then there is absolutely no
need for you!
But you wanna know what I did today?
Husband I prayed for you! Something I have not
done in a very long time.
It came out of nowhere, and I am glad it did.
It reminded me not to settle, but to wait for you!
I know you are going to be everything God needs
you to be for me!
How can you be so sure?
Because God told me!

Chapter 7

*There is someone equipped
to carry you*

"Breathe in, breathe out. Breathe in breathe out."

This is what I tell myself on a day to day basis. Some days I feel so hopeless. As you can imagine from my very lengthy poem. Poetry is a way that I freely express myself. Some days I am very hopeful, other days I have no hope at all. After being single for as long as I have, you began to wonder if there anyone out there for me. I want to reassure you there is someone equipped to carry you. I know you may be tired of waiting, so am I, but do not settle. He is coming!

I do not know when. But what I am sure of, is that I have had my share of failed relationships. I would rather wait longer than marry wrong. Surely, I am supposed to be married by now, I did all the wifely things. I showed what I thought to be love. Which was really manipulation dressed up in a fancy suit. I had submission down pact, even if they did not. I would cook, clean, iron just as expected. I was doing all the right things, just the wrong timing. Little did I know pretending was preparing me to be a great wife. Whomever I was with at the time, I catered to their every need. I always had a hot home-cooked meal prepared. The house was always spic and span. What more could a guy ask for right? My all still was not enough. You will never be good enough for the wrong one. Some days I think maybe I have been through too much for one to handle.

It was snowing outside, and it was cold. I needed a ride to the grocery store. I did not have a car at the time, nor gas money to pay anyone. I was not accustomed to being without a car. Depending on other people left me carless and walking. Knowing my baby had to eat, I wrapped him up and headed to the store. It was then I said I will never allow myself to be this low again. I was broke, homeless, carless, and walking with a baby on my hip and groceries in the other hand. Going through what I have been through, will make anyone "boss up". It taught me survival skills. Baby if we ever get stuck on an island, we will survive. Not only did it teach me survival skills, but it also made me tough. I stopped crying all the time, and I gained a backbone. How will you know when you have found the one equipped to carry you? He will compliment you. Not make you whole, because you should already be whole, that is not his job. Make sure you and your future spouse can build together. Can you advance the kingdom together? What will you create as one?

I refuse to marry someone, just because I love them. You can fall in love with anyone, but you cannot fall into purpose with everyone. Someone may have the potential to be a great husband or a great wife, but if that is all they have that will quickly fade. I believe we should marry more than a person's potential. Choosing potential leads to disappointment when the potential does not meet expectations years into the relationship. A person can be full of hope and potential but going nowhere fast. It is great for a person to be full of ambition however if they are not doing anything with that ambition, it is like a wasted fire consuming everything in its reach. Two people must have common goals in common or it will not work!

You will soon find yourself depressed, frustrated and miserable trying to bring that person to your standards. It does not matter how much you love them. Loving someone does not mean you are supposed to be married to them. The thing you think is best for you could turn out to be the worst thing for you. Marriage is supposed to be forever, no one wants to spend their entire marriage trying to bring their mate up to speed. The best thing we can do when choosing our spouse is to hear the voice of God. And remember marriage is a choice! God gives us free will. Do not marry for the sake of it being the right thing to do. Or because your family feels that a person is a good fit for you. Do what is best for you, because at the end of the day, you will spend the rest of your life with that person, not your family. It is your decision, choose wisely. Allow your head to choose for you, and not solely rely on your heart.

Chapter 8

Saving It

Being single can seem like such a long journey, well I know it has been for me. Single eight years and celibate four years and counting. My God, I am ready. No, I do not want to talk about it. Just kidding, that is the whole point of the book. (sings) "I think you want these goodies, bet you thought about it, if you are looking for these goodies keep on looking cause they stay in the jarrrr… Woah woah woah woah."

Sorry yall, I had a moment. R&B artist Ciara sang it best, she said if you are looking for the goodies, keep on looking cause they stay in the jar. Do not turn the page on me yet. I know, I know, saving it until marriage in today's society, is not the most popular thing to do. However, it is the safest and healthiest thing to do, concerning your spiritual compacity as well as your life. According to a new report from the World Health Organization in 2015, more than 3.7 billion people under the age of 50 about 67% of the global population are infected with herpes simplex virus type 1. That are a lot of people. In addition to sexually transmitted diseases, when you have sex with a person, you all become one flesh. Well, I do not want to become one with anyone else except my husband. God wants us to honor Him with our bodies.

"Do you not know that your bodies are temples of the Holy Spirit, who is in you, whom you have received from God? You are not your own; you were bought at a price. Therefore, honor God with your bodies." 1 Corinthians 6:19-20

"Keaires that's good and all but what do you expect me to do? I have needs."

Yes, you are exactly right! We all have needs. That is how God designed us. Sex was never meant to be a bad thing. The enemy perverted it. Sex was designed to be between husband and wife. It was designed to seal the marriage. So, yes, saving it until marriage is God's way of doing it. If you have a problem with masturbation, or cannot seem to stop having sex, do not I repeat do not beat yourself up. Did you know when we constantly tell ourselves not to do something, or we guilt trip or shame ourselves, or allow the enemy to shame us it makes us want to sin more. We begin to feel as if we have already messed up, so we may as well keep going. Sometimes our body is just doing its natural due diligence.

When a woman ovulates, her body releases an egg from her ovaries. Your hormones are all over the place, and you have a strong desire to have sex. That is normal. Some foods even increase your sex drive. Walnuts improve the quality of sex, coffee spikes your sex drive. (Fun Fact for all my coffee drinkers out there.) Spinach, avocados, celery, and many other "healthy" foods that we are encouraged to eat by doctors. Prayerfully what I am about to share with you sets you free and keeps you free. I am also preaching to myself here if you have accepted Jesus Christ as your Lord and Savior then what I am about to share applies to you.

THERE IS NO CONDEMNATION! YOU HAVE BEEN FORGIVEN OF ALL YOUR SINS AND YOU ARE RIGHTEOUS!

There I said it. Stop beating yourself up. Jesus died for all your sins, past, future and present. His blood was enough to cover your sins. By Faith, through Jesus Christ you are justified! Repeat these words over your life every day. I am righteous, I am Holy, I am justified. The more I spoke this over my life, the less these areas became a struggle for me. As long as I was guilt tripping and shaming myself, I kept falling. If you tell yourself do not have sex, do not masturbate, do not think about it. You are going to do just that. Because you fell, or happen to fall, does not make you any less saved than the person who attends church, or the woman that sits beside you in church with the long skirt down to her ankles. You are still saved!

If my son smacks somebody, he doesn't stop being my son, because he smacked somebody, he is still my son. Same with us and God. Just because we fall, that doesn't make us any less of a daughter or son, we will still be children of God, even after the fall. When you find yourself focusing on something so much, it becomes your reality. People who say I am so broke, nothing ever goes right for me. They have shaped their reality. When you see them, they are indeed broke, and nothing is going right for them. Know your triggers. What are your triggers? I cannot Netflix and chill with nobody that I am not the least bit attracted to. Certain movies, certain music bring back old memories for me. Do not place yourself in situations where you are bound to fall. Make this thing as easy as possible for you. Try not to focus so much on what you should not be doing. Focus on what you should be doing. Focus on who and what God says you are. In Romans 8:37 God says you are more than a conquer. Deuteronomy 28:13 tells us we are the head and not the tail, you are above and not beneath. He says you are the apple of his eye. He loves you and he is not mad at you. I don't care if you slept with somebody last night. God still loves you, and you have been forgiven. You are not waiting for forgiveness. Jesus was the ultimate sacrifice. He paid it all. You are not condemned. No matter what man says. If you go into the grocery and the cashier rings up all your food, you pull out your money to pay, and she says it's already been paid. You're not going to say hey take my money, I want to pay for it anyway. No! It has already been paid! That my friend is grace! That is Jesus and the love that he has for us. The grace of God triumphs any and all sin. Is Grace the key to keep sinning? Of course not, but it is the cure. (Spoken by Joseph Prince)

Once you find yourself meditating on what God says and speaking those things over your life. Sin will be so far away from your mind, that it will no longer be a struggle. If you are trying to stay strong and save it by yourself I guarantee you will fall every time. Ask me how I know?

"It's yours. It's yours."

"I'll never leave."

"My body belongs to you."

And all the other dumb stuff we say when we get caught up in the moment. Yes, I have been there done that! Had I known what I was announcing over my life, I would have kept quiet. I hate when a flesh-tie tries to rear its ugly head. Maybe you can't seem to stop thinking about a person. They are always on your mind. You try to leave them alone, but you can't. More than likely you have the "I can't leave him alone syndrome". You know no matter what he does, even if it hurts you to the core, you still cannot leave him alone. If you have dealt with an unhealthy relationship or dealing with one now we are about to break that thing in Jesus name! You must first and foremost make up in your mind you are willing and ready to leave her or him alone. Remember everything we do starts with a thought. Okay, let's dive in. Begin to think of names of people you have slept with and promised them it was theirs forever. I know for some of you this may require some work. But we will get through this. I have attached a prayer below.

Pray this prayer out loud over your life:

I _insert your name here)_ renounce all covenants, pacts, promises, curses, sexual dealings, emotional dealings and all dealings with _(insert person you are breaking the attachment_. To whom which I have been exposed to or made liable to by my own actions or by the actions of others. I come out of agreement with all ungodly relationships in Jesus name. I break them off my life now! I command my thoughts to line up with the will of God for my life. Where I have been broken, Lord I ask that you go in and restore me. I decree that I am free from the bondage of man, and I declare it to be so now. Shame will no longer haunt and torment me. I am free from what I did and who I did it with. I desire to live in a manner that is pleasing to you Lord. Strengthen me on this new-found journey. Keep me from what's hurting me. God your word says no weapon formed against me shall prosper. I plead the blood of Jesus over my life. I decree I am free! And I declare it to be so now. I am a new creature in Christ. And I am made whole. In Jesus name, I do pray. I believe if you just prayed this prayer over your life with a sincere heart. Get ready to see the manifestations.

Poem Alabaster box

I decided what's in my alabaster box was too
expensive to continue giving away.
So I made the decision to wait.
I was not forced, but more so loved into the idea of
waiting.
God did not condemn me because I gave it away
once upon a time. But showed me I was special to
him and worth the wait.
He showed me what's inside of my alabaster box
should be reserved for my King!
And that love should not be awakened before it's
time.

Chapter 9

From the Beginning

As I sat in the police car in a daze, watching them pick him up off the ground and throw him into the police car. My mind began to run wild with thoughts of going to prison.

"What would it be like?"

"I am not prison material."

"Those women are going to tear me to shreds."

I began to cry all over again at the thought of being locked up. The male policeman got into the car with me.

Wham! He hit the dashboard hard with his hand. It scared me out of the daze I was in. He began to yell at me in his deep masculine voice,

"How old are you"? "Let me see your ID". "Why are you here with this low life?" "Do you have nothing to live for?" "I should charge you with harboring a fugitive."

Which he had every right to. I was harboring fugitive. Even though it was not my house. I knew the police were looking for him. I knew he had committed murder the previous night before.

"Give me one good reason why I should not take you to prison."

I responded with tears in my eyes, "Because I have a son who needs me."

It was at that moment I realized, my son needed me. Sitting in that police car was the start of a new life for me. God graced me with my freedom. I was able to walk away, with no prison time and not a visible scratch on me. But there were scratches on my heart, from when I saw the police car pull off with Twan. I felt like a piece of me left too. I can honestly say God single handily erased each and every scratch. What does any of this have to do with becoming a wife? Well, my experiences built me, they helped shaped me. I have overcome many obstacles in life. I am a new creature in Christ. I love me, and I know who I am. The pain I went through birthed purpose in me. In the end, it all worked out for my good. Maybe you have dealt with something similar. Staying mad and bitter only gives the enemy more power.

"For we wrestle not against flesh and blood, but against principalities, against powers, against the rulers of the darkness of this world, against spiritual wickedness in high places." Ephesians 6:12 KJV

Turn your pain into success. Allow your pain to push you! And most importantly never give up! Do not allow your past to shame you, and make you think that you are not a wife! Everything that you have read has molded me into the woman I am today.

I am living my life, not missing a beat. I know it is only higher from here.

Dear future husband when you find me, I want you to know I was a wife before you found me....

Epilogue

You have a collect call from an inmate at the Alabama Department of Corrections. Do you accept these charges...

About the Author

Keaires Roberson is a native of Sheffield, Alabama. She is a lover of Christ and a firm believer of His word. In her spare time, she loves to sing, cook, act and write poetry. Keaires obtained a degree in Social Science from John C. Calhoun Community College. She currently resides in Huntsville, Alabama with her son Jaden.

Made in the USA
Columbia, SC
25 February 2025